I0407937

DONKEY COLORING BOOK

Coloring Book for Adults Containing 30 Hand Drawn, Paisley, Henna and Zentangle Donkey Coloring Pages

ISBN-13: 978-1546351214
ISBN-10: 1546351213

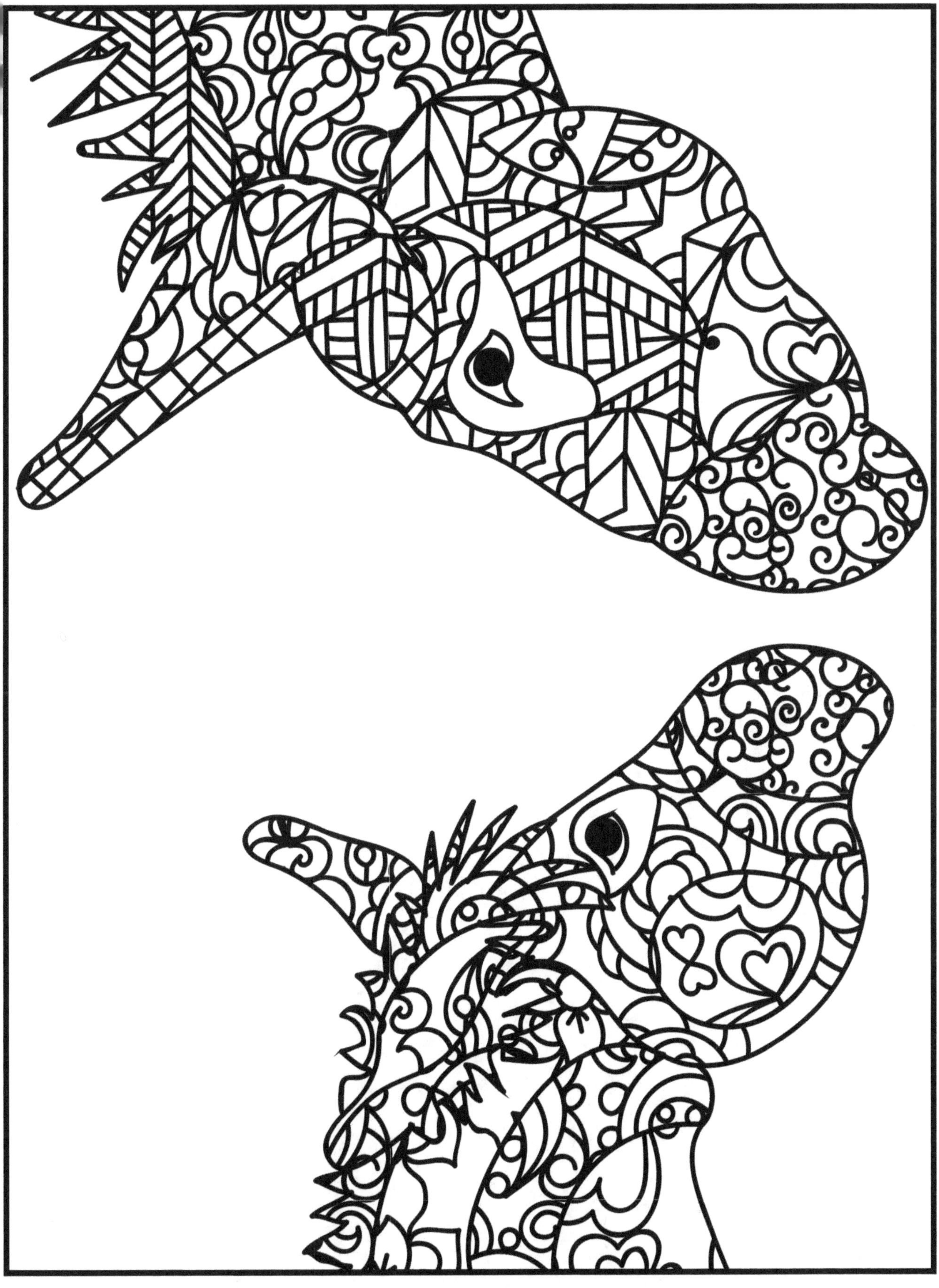

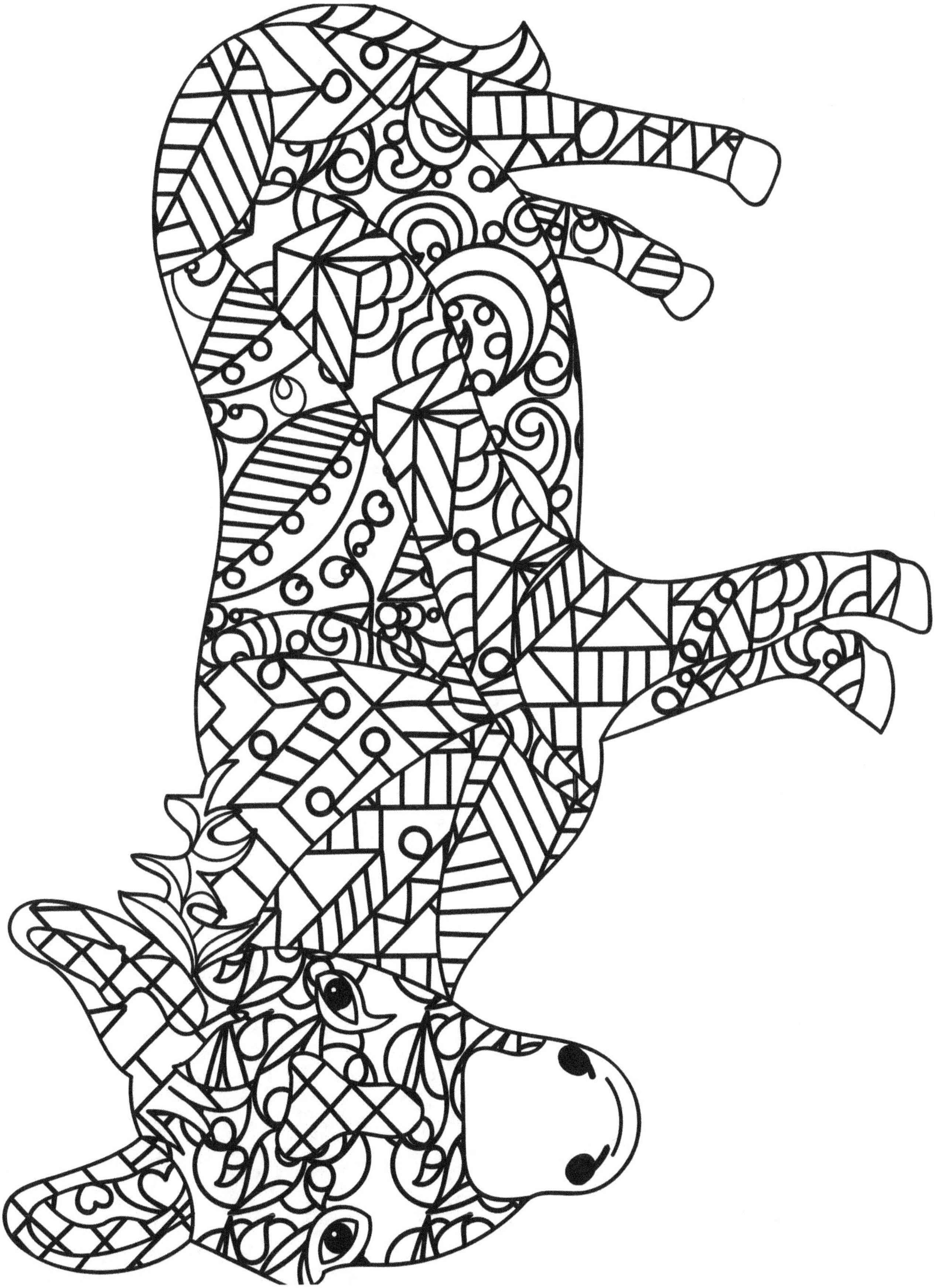

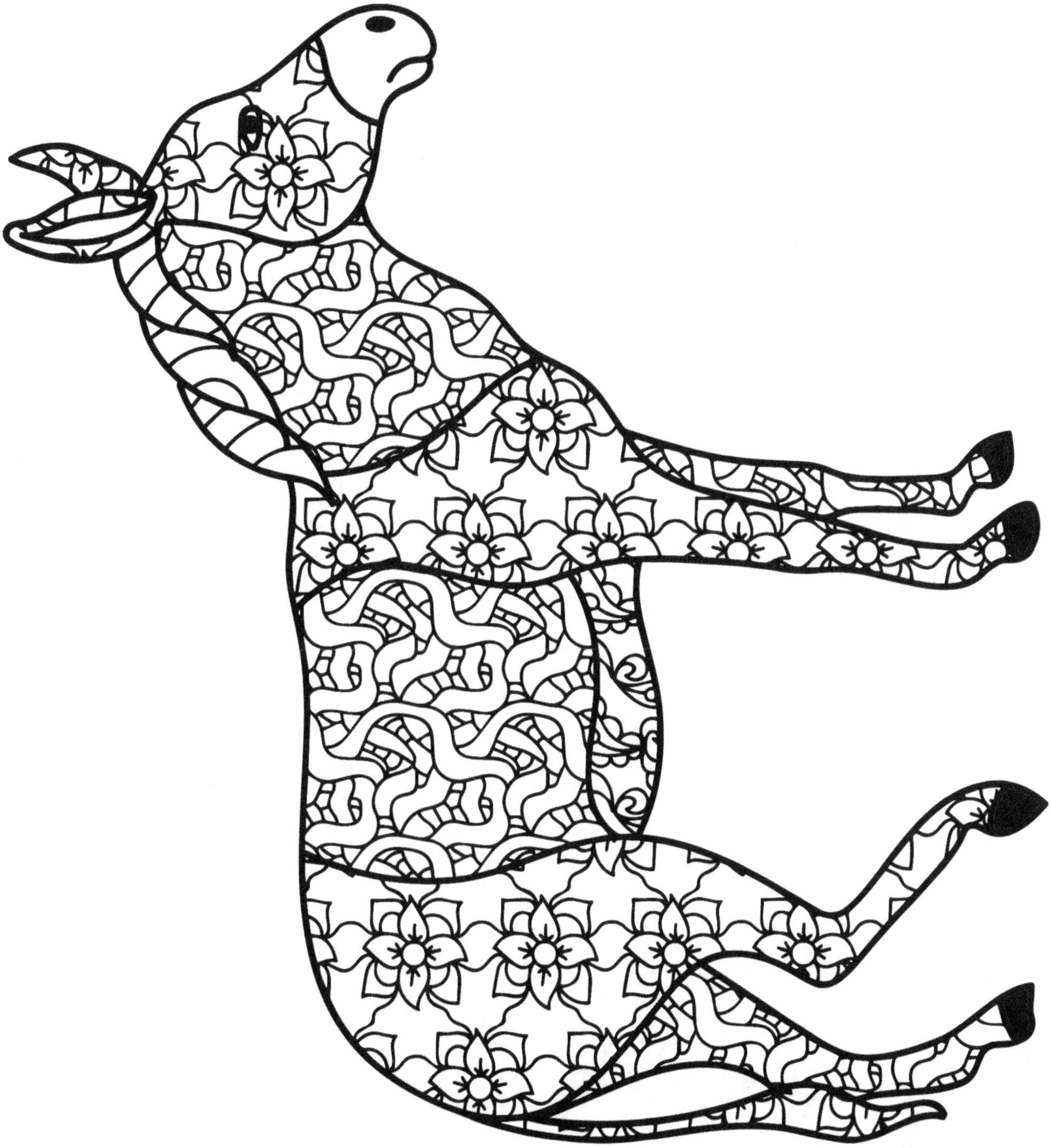

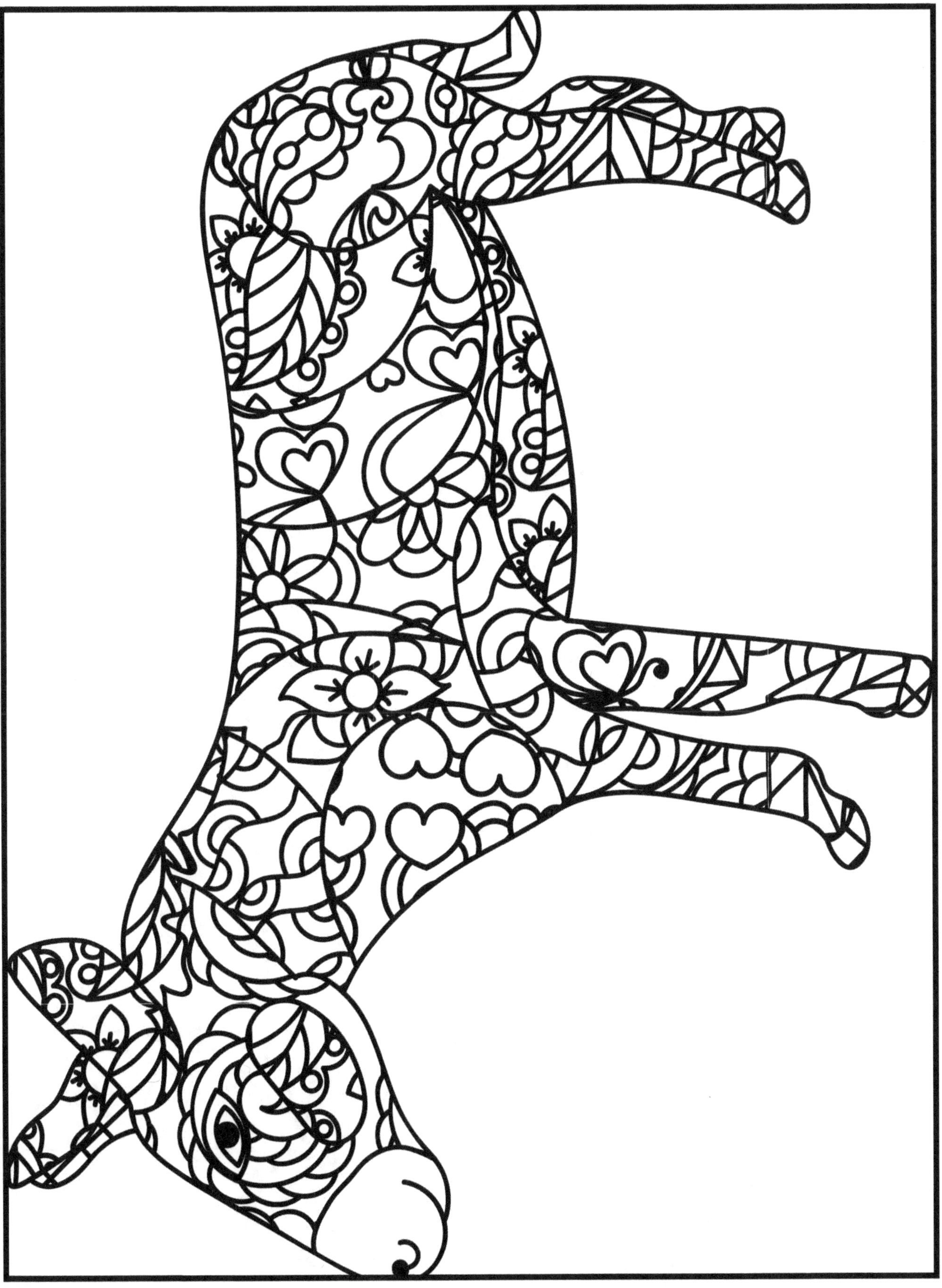

www.ingramcontent.com/pod-product-compliance
Lightning Source LLC
Chambersburg PA
CBHW081418280526
45788CB00009B/3151
* 9 7 8 1 5 4 6 3 5 1 2 1 4 *